Careers in Self-Driving Car Technology

Martin Gitlin

Published in the United States of America by
Cherry Lake Publishing, Ann Arbor, Michigan
www.cherrylakepublishing.com

Reading Adviser: Marla Conn, MS, Ed., Literacy specialist, Read-Ability, Inc.

Photo Credits: Cover, chombosan; page 4 (left), eHrach; Page 4 (right), Riksa Prayogi; page 6, REDPIXEL.PL; page 8, Alexey Ryazonov; page 10, Pincasso; page 12, Trong Nguyen: page 14, wavebreakmedia; page 16, kurhan; page 18, Scharfsinn: page 20, Zapp2Photo; page 22, Zapp2Photo; page 24, Scharfsinn; page 26, supparson; page 28, Chesky. Source: Shutterstock.

Library of Congress Cataloging-in-Publication Data

CIP data has been filed and is available at catalog.loc.gov.

Printed in the United States of America.

Table of Contents

Hello, Emerging Tech Careers!

In the past ...

Groundbreaking inventions made life easier in many ways.

In the present ...

New technologies are changing the world in mind-boggling ways.

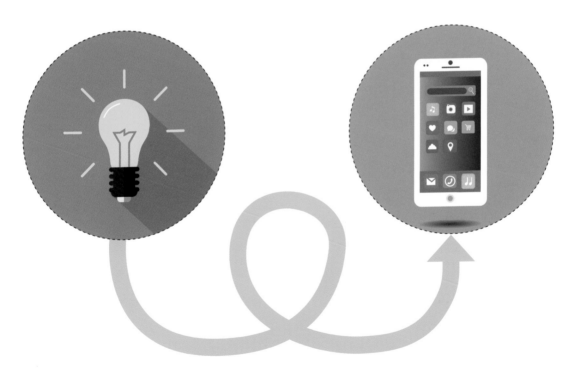

The future is yours to imagine!

WHAT COMES NEXT?

Who would have thought?

Alexander Graham Bell invented the first telephone in 1876.
In 1879, Thomas Edison invented the first electric lightbulb.
The Wright brothers successfully flew the first airplane in 1903.
And don't forget Henry Ford! He invented a way to make cars
quicker and cheaper.

These brilliant inventors did things that people once thought
were impossible. To go from candles to electricity? From
horse-drawn carriages to automobiles and airplanes? Wow!

The sky's the limit!

Now technology is being used to do even more amazing things!
Take **self-driving cars**, for instance. Yes, you read that right—
cars that drive themselves! People are working to perfect cars
that are driven by robotic technology instead of humans. Some
say this could be safer and more efficient than human drivers.
After all, **robots** don't text and drive!

This book explores the people and professions behind self-driving
cars. Some of these careers, like sensor software engineer, are
so cutting-edge that they didn't exist just a decade or so ago. Others,
like mechanic, offer exciting new twists using this technology.

Read on to explore exciting possibilities for your future!

Car Designer

You are in a car. It can be anywhere on the road. A cool-looking vehicle pulls up next to you. Your heart beats a little faster. Your eyes open a little wider. You love how the car is designed. That is exactly the reaction car designers wanted from you. It is also the reaction that has inspired many people to become car designers.

Car design is a career of passion. People are driven to design because they love cool-looking cars. It is a job they dream about. Perhaps they sketched out designs as kids. Or they imagined new designs in their minds. To make their dream a reality, they must learn about **computer-aided design** and engineering.

Those who combine their passion with artistic talent will succeed in car design. They create new ideas that must also be practical. They work with engineers to ensure their designs can be turned into functioning vehicles. The designs must appeal to the public. But the car they create must also be affordable.

Cars designers require many traits beyond **creativity**. They must have strong math and science skills. They need talent in computer-aided drafting, which is technical drawing. This is true for designing traditional and self-driving cars. A wide variety of sizes and designs have been used to make self-driving cars come to life.

Imagine It!

➔ Pretend you are the designer of the first self-driving school bus.

➔ You have to consider safety and keep the riders entertained and supervised.

➔ Now draw the coolest self-driving school bus you can imagine.

Dig Deeper!

✔ Click on the following website that details how cars are designed: https://www.toyota.co.jp/en/kids/car/design.html.

✔ Using what you learned, write down the three coolest aspects of car design. Then explain why you chose them.

Every detail of a car—inside and outside—is thoughtfully designed.

Car designers are artists. They work in an artistic environment. Their studios feature all the tools of the trade. The design process begins with ideas discussed with engineers and other designers. They sketch out ideas on paper with markers, chalk, and colored pencils. They use **3D** computer modeling programs, as well as illustration programs such as Photoshop, Paint, and Illustrator.

Their designs are printed out in large sizes. They are studied, improved, and finalized. They are then taken to managers or directors within the car companies.

Sometimes car designers compete against each other. That competition can be fierce. Companies compare designs and pick the one they like best. That can be a nervous time for designers. They fear that all their hard work will be for nothing. But even in defeat, they maintain their love for car design, just like when they were kids.

Future Car Designer

Most car companies hire designers with a bachelor's or master's degree in product or automotive design. Important courses include electrical engineering, math, and computer-aided drafting. The field is competitive. That means companies are looking for top students. Landing an internship is a great first step.

Mapping Engineer

Not long ago, when drivers got lost, they had to stop to ask someone for directions. Or they might unfold a large map. Global positioning system (GPS) tools have all but ended that problem. But how would a self-driving car keep from getting lost? How does it know where to go? Welcome to the job of the mapping engineer.

It is amazing that cars can go places without a driver. It would be more amazing if they knew where to travel without being told. But that is impossible. They do not read minds. They are like robots that need directions.

Mapping engineers use computer vision to build **high-definition** (HD) maps for self-driving cars. The vehicles are programmed to go where they are supposed to go. But that is not the first step in the process. Mapping engineers must wait for mappers to do their jobs.

Companies hire thousands of mappers, who install a special device in their own cars. It is placed on the windshield just above the rearview mirror. The mappers drive slowly on streets all around the world. The device uses a combination of lasers and radar. These read everything on the road—traffic signals, lane markers, and street signs. They read whatever self-driving cars need in order to know when and where to turn. This information is used to create detailed maps for the cars.

Imagine It!

→ Think about a store or restaurant you often visit.

→ Draw your own map to that place. Use arrows to indicate turns and images to mark landmarks that will help you find your way.

→ Use your map the next time your family goes there. Is it accurate?

Dig Deeper!

✓ List every detail on your street without looking. Write down every fire hydrant, tree, and telephone pole.

✓ Take a walk down your street with your list. Did you miss anything?

Mapping engineers must capture every detail of busy roadways.

Mapping engineers begin their jobs when mappers have completed theirs. They receive the data from mappers. They take that data and run advanced computer vision systems to map the roads. The HD maps are precise. They detail the location of such landmarks as traffic lights and turning lanes down to 1 inch (2.5 centimeters). They even mark fire hydrants and the height of grass on the side of the road!

Companies around the world that want to test self-driving cars hire mapping engineers. Among them are carmakers like General Motors and taxi or delivery services such as Uber.

Mapping engineers and technicians work in many different areas, not just on self-driving cars. They convert paper maps to digital ones. They collect data for miners. They create maps to determine the best spots for housing developments. But self-driving cars have provided a new and exciting opportunity.

Future Mapping Engineer

It is no surprise that mapping engineers need to have an engineering degree. Not every college offers specific courses in mapping engineering. But jobs in mapping engineering can be attained with degrees in other areas, such as computer engineering and mechanical engineering. Mapping engineers must be well-versed in computer science and math.

Mechanic

Mechanics still repair cars with wrenches, hammers, screwdrivers, and pliers. But the emergence of self-driving cars will result in some changes to their duties. Mechanics capable of fixing and maintaining such advanced vehicles will be in demand. So will the experts who can train them.

The only tools auto mechanics once used could be held in one hand. Problems could be found using just their eyes and their experience. Times have changed. Electric cars, which use no gas, are on the road. **Diagnostic** equipment is required nowadays to detect issues with cars. Mechanics often turn to computers to find the best fix.

Advanced technology will not end the need for mechanics. The biggest difference between self-driving cars and traditional cars is that one is driven by a person and the other is not. Self-driving cars still have brakes, steering wheels, and other parts that can fail. They will still need oil changes and coolants. Those issues will always require mechanics. Self-driving cars do feature **futuristic** parts not found in traditional cars. These include lasers, radar, and **sensors**.

Cars are not the only self-driving vehicles that will still need mechanics. Companies are producing self-driving

Imagine It!

- Pretend you are a car mechanic.

- Look under the hood of a family car.

- See if you can identify at least three parts.

Dig Deeper!

- Click on the following website: http://bit.ly/carpartsforkids.

- Write down five new facts about cars that you discover.

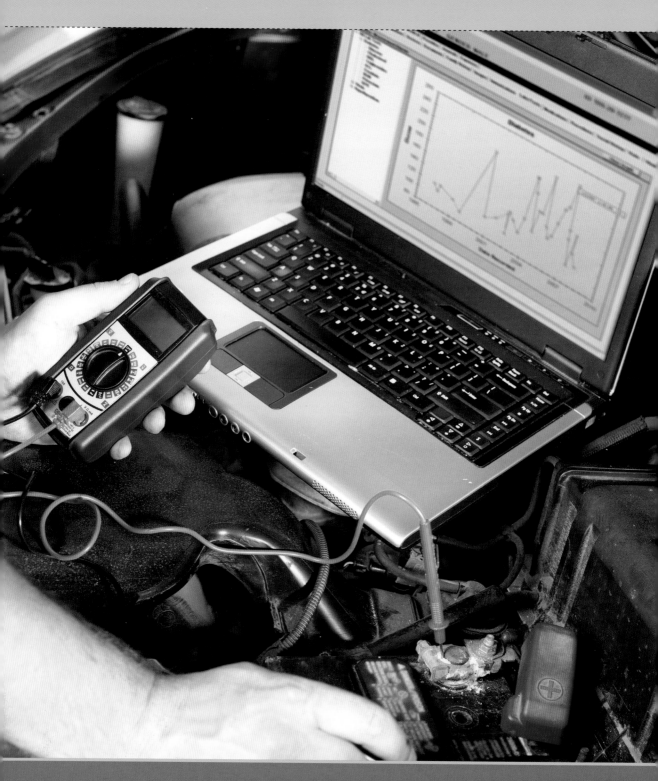

Repairing self-driving cars requires high-tech skills.

trucks. These save gas money and give drivers a break during long trips around the country. Traditional truck drivers will still be hired. They might take over the wheel in bad weather and in stop-and-go city driving.

More mechanics will be trained to fix self-driving trucks. They will need to learn about the advanced technology that requires special service.

Traditional mechanics will still be needed for issues such as flat tires and fluid changes. But there is a need for technicians who can master the digital technology involved in fixing self-driving cars and trucks. Vehicles are changing with the times. Mechanics must do so as well.

Future Mechanics

Mechanics and auto technicians are most often high school graduates. Many complete a program in automotive technology. They receive training at a vocational or technical school. Some learn at community colleges or universities. High schools often offer car repair and maintenance courses.

Safety Driver

In 2016, a taxi service called Uber started testing self-driving cars on the roads of San Francisco. One of its self-driving vehicles ran a red light. Others were involved in minor accidents. Nobody was hurt. Uber was not blamed for the crashes. But the company had not proven that its self-driving cars were safe.

The idea of self-driving cars scares some people. What if they encounter something unexpected? Like a traffic jam. Or an icy, slippery road. Or an accident that leaves other vehicles in odd places. Or a police car swerving from one lane to another to catch a speeder. How do self-driving cars know how to avoid contact? Safety drivers make sure they do.

Safety is the most important quality of a self-driving car. That means safety drivers are important as well. They test cars to make sure they are safe.

Safety drivers sit in self-driving cars at test facilities. They watch carefully as the cars steer around grassy mounds and parked cars. The cars are confronted by obstacles. Doors of parked cars fly open as they approach. **Mannequins** jaywalk in front of them. Safety drivers evaluate the performance of the cars. They make certain the vehicles can handle whatever real people and real traffic will throw at them. And they take control in case of emergency.

Imagine It!

- ➔ The next time you are a passenger in a car, pretend you are a safety driver.

- ➔ Imagine a steering wheel in your hands.

- ➔ Make every turn the driver makes on the way to your destination.

Dig Deeper!

- ✔ What are some rules you can think of about keeping kids safe in cars?

- ✔ Make a chart you can use to share with younger children.

Safety drivers perform test drives to see how well self-driving cars perform in real traffic situations.

Safety drivers take a series of tests driving regular cars before they operate a self-driving car. Those who pass then begin a training course. That entails classroom instruction, exams, and supervised driving at a test track and on the roads.

A company called Waymo began testing self-driving cars with no safety driver inside in 2017. It remains to be seen if those tests will lead to others.

Companies that produce self-driving cars claim they will someday be safer than driver-controlled cars. But they also admit that such a time remains in the future. Until then, they will take no chances. Safety drivers will be required until self-driving cars are proven to be completely safe.

Future Safety Drivers

Safety drivers need no background in robotics or engineering. They are not required to earn a college degree. But they do need a driver's license and a clean driving record, which means no arrests. They must undergo a series of tests and training courses to make sure they can handle the job.

Sensor Software Engineer

We have five senses: sight, hearing, touch, taste, and smell. People use most of these senses to drive, especially sight and hearing. Self-driving cars don't have eyes and ears. But they are equipped with "senses" called **sensors**. Sensor software engineers make sure of that.

People use vision more than any other sense when they drive. They use their eyes to detect stop signs, red lights, and other cars' turn signals. Their eyes also focus on any unusual problems that force them to suddenly shift directions.

Software engineers develop and install software systems in self-driving cars to make them safe. The sensors in the cars "tell" them to stop when they approach other cars. Or to move forward when the red light becomes green. Or to wait to turn at a stop sign.

The technology for self-driving cars is still in its infancy. But sensor software engineers use their experience, computer skills, and knowledge to develop new ideas. They then refine those ideas. Only when they are satisfied with their software systems will they place them into self-driving cars. Those systems must be trusted to improve safety and performance. Vehicle testing on test tracks and roads determine how well their sensor software is working.

Imagine It!

➡ Make a list (or draw pictures) of all the ways you used your senses today.

Dig Deeper!

✔ Use your favorite Internet search engine (like Google) to find out all you can about "self-driving car sensors."

✔ Make a chart naming each one you discover and describing what it does.

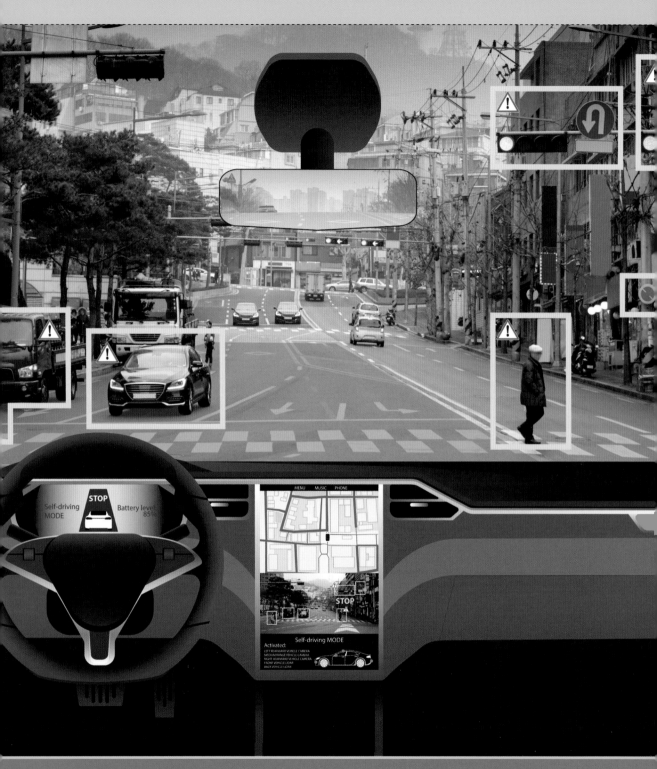

Sensor software engineers program self-driving cars with sensors that mimic a human's five senses.

One of their tasks is to develop, design, and put into use drive-by-wire systems. Those are electronic or computer systems that replace traditional ones in cars. Typical cars have mechanical parts that allow drivers to control their speed and direction. Drive-by-wire systems allow self-driving cars to brake and steer on their own.

Sensor software engineers do not only work on self-driving cars. They also work on unmanned spacecraft such as **drones**. They might work on developing sensors for cameras. Their talents are valuable to a variety of industries.

But self-driving cars are the wave of the future. And sensor software engineers will be critical to their success.

Future Sensor Software Engineers

Someone seeking a career as a sensor software engineer must be good at computer science and math. A college degree in computer science is preferred. Some companies demand that their job candidates have a master's degree. They also look for those with some software development experience.

Vehicle Trainer

Perhaps someday you will see people sitting in cars with no drivers. It is quite possible they will not be there simply to enjoy the ride or the scenery. The passengers might very well be self-driving vehicle trainers.

It is easy to know how people are behaving. Their actions and words give them away. But it is much harder to detect how a self-driving car is behaving. A quiet ride might be masking a major problem. That is why self-driving car companies hire vehicle trainers. They are experts in automotive behavior. They understand what makes self-driving cars healthy and what makes them sick. They **evaluate** software with the vehicle in motion.

Vehicle trainers also challenge their cars. They test them in rain and snow, on hilly and twisting roads, on long distances, and in stop-and-go driving. They know that their self-driving cars must be able to handle all conditions.

Vehicle trainers work in teams. They take turns observing how the vehicle behaves while they're inside the car. They watch how the car reacts as it drives itself. Sometimes the trainers are forced to take over behind the wheel. They must remain calm under pressure if an emergency arises.

Imagine It!

→ What is something you are really good at doing?

→ Put together a how-to demonstration to train others how to do it as well as you do.

→ Use a smartphone to record your presentation.

Dig Deeper!

● The next time you are a passenger in a car, pay attention to all the decisions the driver has to make.

● Keep a tally of how many stops, turns, and other actions the driver takes to get from one place to another.

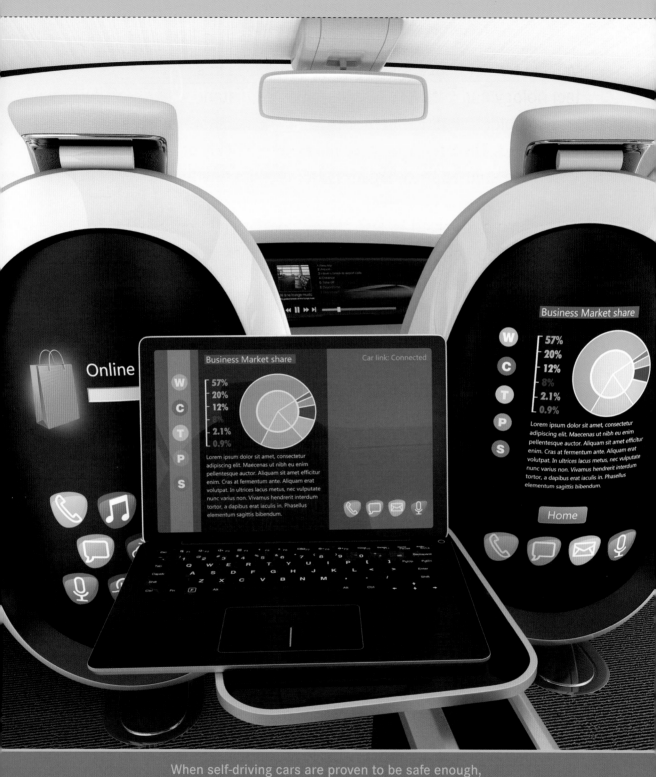

When self-driving cars are proven to be safe enough,
human drivers can sit back and enjoy the ride!

Vehicle trainers have been trained as experts in self-driving car technology and software. They travel long distances to carefully and completely test their cars. They then detail how the cars have performed. Their reports must be written quickly on a computer. These are studied by operations and engineering teams.

All problems reported by vehicle trainers are addressed. They must be fixed before the cars are put into service. Vehicle trainers are trusted to accurately assess any problems.

Learning all about self-driving cars is not the first step to becoming a vehicle trainer. They must first have a spotless driving record. They must also understand that their workplace is the road. Vehicle trainers do not spend much time in the comfort of their own homes. But they have jobs that play a big part in the future of the car industry.

Future Vehicle Trainer

Companies that hire vehicle trainers might prefer college graduates. They might only hire those with knowledge of advanced automotive technology, though it might not be required. However, a willingness to learn all about self-driving cars is a must.

Can You Imagine?

Innovation always starts with an idea. This was true for Alexander Graham Bell, Thomas Edison, Henry Ford, and the Wright brothers. It is still true today as innovators imagine new forms of self-driving cars. And it will still be true in the future when you begin your high-tech career. So ...

What is your big idea?

Think of a cool way to use self-driving cars. Write a story or draw a picture to share your idea with others.

Please do **NOT** write in this book if it doesn't belong to you.
Gather your own paper and art supplies and get creative with your ideas!

Glossary

computer-aided design (kuhm-PYOO-tur eyd-id dih-ZINE) the process of creating plans and drawings on a computer to develop the design of something

creativity (kree-ay-TIV-ih-tee) the ability to make new things or think of new ideas

diagnostic (dye-uhg-NAH-stik) a routine for testing a piece of hardware or for locating an error in a computer program

drones (DROHNZ) unmanned aircraft guided by remote control or onboard computers

evaluate (ih-VAL-yoo-ate) to judge or determine the significance, worth, or quality of something

futuristic (fyoo-chur-IS-tik) having or involving very modern technology or design

high-definition (HYE-def-uh-NISH-uhn) a high degree of detail in an image or screen

innovations (in-uh-VAY-shuhnz) new ideas or inventions

mannequins (MAN-ih-kinz) dummies used to represent humans

self-driving cars (SELF-DRIVE-ing KAHRZ) robotic vehicles designed to travel between destinations without human operators

sensors (SEN-surz) devices that detect and respond to some type of input from the physical environment

Index

About the Author

Martin Gitlin is a freelance author based in Cleveland. He has had more than 110 books published. He won more than 45 writing awards during his 11 years as a newspaper journalist, including first place for general excellence from the Associated Press. That organization selected him as one of the top four feature writers in Ohio in 2001.